INSTEAD OF A.

Geoff Hattersley has been publishing and performing his poetry since 1984. His work has been widely published and has been used as part of syllabuses in schools, universities, and with The Open University. He edited The Wide Skirt Press from 1986 until 1998, publishing 30 issues of the magazine and 24 books and pamphlets. He lives in Huddersfield with his wife Jeanette.

Also by Geoff Hattersley

Port of Entry (Littlewood Press, 1989)

Don't Worry (Bloodaxe Books, 1994)

'On the Buses' with Dostoyevsky (Bloodaxe Books, 1998)

Harmonica (Wrecking Ball Press, 2003)

Back of Beyond (Smith Doorstop, 2006)

Outside the Blue Hebium (Smith Doorstop, 2012)

Instead of an Alibi

Geoff Hattersley

Broken Sleep Books

ISBN: 978-1-915760-38-8

Cover designed by Aaron Kent

Edited & Typeset by Aaron Kent

Broken Sleep Books Ltd
Rhydwen
Talgarreg
Ceredigion
SA44 4HB

Broken Sleep Books Ltd
Fair View
St Georges Road
Cornwall
PL26 7YH

Contents

NEW THING

The Nation's Favourite Poems

LONELY AS A CROWD

New Thing

New Thing

It came out of thin air, out of nowhere.
Once it was here, no one could imagine
how the days had gone by before, to what purpose.

Old habits die hard was found to be wrong.
New Thing was what no one could avert their gaze from.
Rockets were fired; fortunes were made, lost, and made again.

One little girl drew a picture of it that won a prize.
A guitarist composed a symphony, got an award.
No one saw the picture, nor heard the symphony,

they were too busy with it, the new thing.
New Thing seduced people, collected them.
It knew it would always be the new thing.

Motions

Like placing a sticking plaster
over a shotgun wound,
we're all wasting our time

with these green bins,
but it keeps some folk happy
to go through the motions.

Here's my contribution,
which includes poetry
to give the bin some soul,

the work of years or
the play of years,
the work and the play being the same thing.

Stuck With It

He looks like he ended up with the face he earned
after smoking opium for ten years
through the oily barrel of a rifle.

There's a whole bunch of thugs riding his bones.
Trying to make sense of it all has worn him down.
Right place, wrong time, no luck, no hope, nothing.

Reckless, stupid, heading for the nearest
meathead magnet, size ten steel toe capped boots
stamping out a stupid, reckless rhythm.

There's an old jazz melody in his head.
Orange was the colour of her dress, then blue silk.
It's good to think of stuff like that at times like this.

Expecting to be Homeless

Looks to me like it's got more snow in it.
That's what he says, peering seriously at the sky.
He stands in six inches of snow and peers.

This new weather won't be much fun when we're homeless.
Let's chill out and listen to Charles Mingus.
I speak his name through what's left of my teeth.

He stands in six inches of snow and peers.
I'll tell thee what, he says, we'll have a drink.
We sit freezing, supping cider, quiet.

There are folk who wish they were dead, but we're not them.
Let's chill out and listen to Mr Ellington.
I speak his name with what's left of my breath.

Straight, No Chaser

What they call a disposable income –
he's not really got one

right now, just a list of things he covets,
like the complete works of Thelonius Monk

on pristine vinyl, and a tin of beans.
Only joking! He's got a tin of beans,

got two. In the cupboard. Next to the peas.
On the shelf between the two empty shelves.

No end to the insults, no end to them.
Don't you worry about me, pal,

I can live on ten pence a bastard day.
And still have something left over.

Instead of an Alibi

He needs an alibi
for every single day of the past forty years
and he's struggling, struggling.

He lights his pipe, inhales –
holds the smoke in till his fat face looks sure to burst
and does, with an encore.

Flicking through his first collection
he's surprised by a decent poem,
tucked away on page 56

like a best pair of shoes
in the bottom of a wardrobe
that's going up in flames.

Grumpy

The train's packed, standing room only.
Everyone's eyes are down, staring dully

into small electronic screens,
their thumbs like pale, agitated creatures –

God's second son
could fly by the window on a winged pig

and not one of them would notice,
not one.

I met someone who could still concentrate
on just one thing for more than one minute,

then I found gold
in the streets of Milnsbridge.

Action

One time I was a computer salesman
who stapled his scrotum to his thigh for a bet
and that wasn't even the stupid bit.

Next thing I was the world's least competent vet.
I got mauled by a lion but survived
long enough to ask for a glass of milk.

I died, often grimly, most of the time.
Strictly bit parts, year after year, shot after shot.
You'll have seen me somewhere, with my sour face.

Now I've been reinvented as a ruthless thug.
The end of the world is round the corner
and everyone has to pay up on time.

After

Seven a.m., the sun already ferocious.
Poking through the remains of last night's barbecue –
someone's guard dog, very tasty.

We banged an old book on the fire -
a man who reads was stoned to death
the other night. No one likes a reader.

I find a pile of pigeons' feet by the cesspit,
hundreds of them. Feathers floating about.
Whoever did it owns a nifty blade.

The search for clean water goes on.
It's the Government's last initiative. I may sign up -
you get an egg and fresh bread every day.

Master of Ceremonies

What tripe some of them come out with.
There's one who wants to be introduced as
the finest love poet of his generation –
seems to expect me to keep a straight face -
and a fat git who aims to outdrink Bukowski,
and at one point will sing a rousing sea shanty.

When young Murphy's blotto cousin
falls off his stool, flat on his face
halfway through a solemn piece
about kissing and touching,
I laugh like mad, the whole room
laughs like mad.
The finest love poet isn't impressed –
tells me off later, the surly fucker.

Next month we have five poets for the price of four.
Thank you all for coming tonight, I hope you enjoyed it.
Thanks especially to the poets themselves.
Let's have one more round of applause.

Hemingway in 10 True Sentences

At the age of eighteen he was blown up
while eating a cheese sandwich.

Sheltering in warm cafes in Paris
he came up with some of his best stories.

After Paris he did the one bad thing
for which he could never forgive himself.

He'd kill a deer, or a brown bear, or a lion
without a second thought.

He'd pick a fight with anyone
if he was sure he could beat them.

He survived two plane crashes in two days
but he wasn't unhurt.

His hair and bushy beard went white
but he didn't look like Father Christmas.

Winning the Nobel Prize for Literature
failed to cheer him up.

He stabbed old friends in the back with a smirk;
electric shock treatments all but finished him off.

Mary found what was left of his head
dripping from the ceiling and walls.

What I'm Up To

Buying a washing machine,
that's what I'm up to.

I've checked out the website
but you really need to see a washer

in the flesh, so to speak.
And here they are - hundreds

of freestanding washing machines,
row upon row, two levels –

washers as far as the eye can –
maybe not hundreds, let's be fair.

They all look the same to me
but the prices vary. I stand and stare at them

like a stuffed cat. My head fills with figures -
load capacity, spin speed, other stuff.

Here comes a salesperson, at last,
a sullen young Asian, face like thunder.

'Can I help you?' he barks.
Must have had a worse night than me.

Knife

Always carry a knife
in case he starts on you,
folk have stabbed him before,
it usually stops him.

Not quite what I wanted
or expected to hear,
my first day on the job,
about to meet the boss.

Waiting For It to Die

He phoned the RSPCA.
They said they'd be eight hours, eight hours at least.
That's great, he thought, just bloody great.
He sat close to the dog on the bloody carpet.

It was conscious, its eyes followed his every move
while its body remained completely still
as a dark pool formed beneath it and spread.
It had hopped in through the open front door and dropped.

Time dragged. A headache hit him hard
as the dog yelped wildly, then fell quiet again.
There was barely any flesh left on its front legs,
just streams of blood down twisted bones.

It was a black and white dog, about three years old.
If he moved his hand toward it, it growled.
The name on its collar was Benjamin.
He sat and watched its eyes lose their sparkle.

Arthur's in Grimsby

He's getting worried
about the weekend –
Arthur's in Grimsby,
Albert's in Thailand.
He could end up
staring at the floor drunk.

He could end up
sitting at a table
eating something
so unhealthy it would scare him
if only he was that little bit
more alert.

He could end up
stuck with someone
who shoots rabbits for fun,
who'll tell him, dead normal,
his ambition's to be an
assassin.

He could end up
with a pile of paper
in front of him,
paper with words on, like
mongoose, tyrant, claptrap,
pedestrian.

Head of Steam

He's the ugliest gravedigger
in the whole of England,
that's his boast anyway,
a well-battered skinhead
growing more dangerous
and stupid with each drink,
a nutcase who could change
your life in an instant.
I'll have to think before
I speak, think twice;
he's already threatened
to smack my face in once,
when I said I didn't care
whether or not Janeway
was a better captain
than Picard and Kirk.

In t' George

1.   Stan and His Lass

Ah've lost mi bastard coyt ageeun
Ah'm allus loyzin' it
In pubs, tha knows, pissed up
Tek it off 'n' forget

Ar lass reckons ah'm mental like
That's a laugh comin' from 'er
Some o' t' stunts shiz pulled o'er t' years
Mad cow!

That time shi come in t' pub
'n' put mi Sunday dinner o'er t' top o' mi 'eeud!
The' we' mashed taties darn t' back o' mi collar
The' we' carrots 'n' sprouts 'n' all soorts

Tha knows what shi reckons meks a good breakfast?
A bleedin' apple
That's all, nowt else, just a bleedin' apple
A bleedin' apple on a bleedin' little plate

2.   *Don's Watter*

Ah remember when ah wa' a young 'un
Ah biked it to 'arrogate
All t' way, non-stop, in t' bloody sun
Abart eleven ah wa'

Ah were deein' o' thust
Ah knocked on a dooer
'n' asked for a drink o' watter
Did ah gerra drink? Did ah 'eck

Ah'll tell thee summat
Tha'd 'ave ter knock
On a lorra bloody dooers in Wombwell
Afore tha farnd someb'dy

That wun't gi' a kid
A drink o' watter
Tha'd 'ave ter knock
On a lorra bloody dooers all reyt

3.   *Sam's Absence from the Horse Shoe Explained*

Ah remember walkin' art o' t' 'oss shoe
This is abart thirty years sin'
Ring Mi Bell wa' on t' juke box
Remember that shite?

Suddenly ah guh flyin'
Ah'm darn on t' floor 'n' ah look up
There's these three lasses in jeans 'n' leather
Stood sneerin' darn at mi

Ah tell thee, ah gorrup 'n' walked art
'n' ah nivver went back ageeun
Ah thought, well, that's enough fer me
If even t' lasses're lookin' fer a feyt nar

It shook mi up a bit ah'll tell thi
It's not like the' w're lads
Wunt raise an eyebrow these days would it?
'n' they'd put t' boot in 'n' all

4.   *Cockroach's Lament*

When ar wa' a young 'un
Resin wa' better 'n' grass
Tha on'y smoouked grass
If tha cun't get nowt else

Tha can't even buy resin ner moor
Not that's any good any rooud
'n' that skunk stuff, ah dun't know
Ah can't be doin' wi' it

Ah'd love a good smoke o' resin though
Afghan black, summat like that
Like it used ter bi, ah meeun, back in t' days
Tha cun't g' wrong wi' that stuff

Thi mind went fuckin' ivvrywheeur
It wa' like all 'n a sudden tha understood stuff
This skunk's nowt like that
Just meks thi even moor mental than tha are already

Iz started writin' stuff tha knows
'ad a couple o' stories in this magazeeun
'e showed it mi, di'n't look like much ter me
But tha'd a thought 'e'd won t' Nobel prize 'r summat

Nar, like, 'e's all lardy da
Dun't even talk ter nob'dy ner moor
Thinks 'e's gunner bi a gret writer
Ah'm not bleedin' jokin'

Ah tell thi, me 'n' thee, wiv got moor chance
O' bein' t' next men on mooin
Gret writer f' fuck's sake!
Livin' in a world o' 'is ooun

Can tha imagine anybody comin' back from t' shop
Carrying a book written by yon?
Ah allus thought 'e wa' a bit 'n a weirdo
Can tha call 'em that these days? Weirdos?

The Painter

He drank alone, just a couple,
checked his pockets for change,
found it fell short.
He heard the landlord say *See you later*
for the last time.

A gentle giant, not quite fifty,
striding in the night air, almost home.

He'd spent his life
in streets like these,
spent his life trying to paint them –
not like a photograph
but as he saw them now,

teeming with life
all the way back
to the days of horses and carts -
strange abstract work
he couldn't sell.

Striding in the night air, almost home,
a gentle giant.

They were in the shadows,
four cheeky lads, asking for fags,
saying *come on, Mister.*
They'd been drinking, having a laugh,
smoking some skunk.

Almost home, a gentle giant.

Called him *a mean old cunt*,
landed a sucker punch,
knocking him off his feet
and out of time, flat out
in the path of a car.

A gentle giant,
gone by the morning.

Perchance

In a slapped hard stupor
with dirty feet

pushing a plough
behind four farting mules

in a field alongside
an electrified fence

at the border
between have and have not

The Nation's Favourite Poems

Norman Writes

You open it, and take it in – it's like
being attacked in broad daylight,
pinned to a wall by a red-faced adolescent
suffering a delusion of omnipotence.

It's no letter, it's a sermon, and if
being preached to by an angry nutter
was something you welcomed, surely
you'd have joined the Southern Baptists.

It pisses on your good humour, ruins
your plans – not very grandiose plans
it's true, but all the same something
you'd been looking forward to for some time.

Wildlife Poem

Taking a smoke at the open window
I spot a big spider, big enough anyway
in a web in the top corner. I love wildlife,

I feel passionate about its preservation,
but I need to mess with spiders
for the horror they've brought into my life.

I blow the smoke straight up at the spider
who gets giddy, falling onto the windowsill,
walking round in circles like a guilty cardinal.

An easy target now. Wish I still had a cat –
Josie gobbled spiders every chance she got.
She chewed with a sour face, legs dangling from her mouth.

Robert Mitchum

Although fans such as I
would argue that numerous films of his
are the sort of films everyone should see,

asked one time which of them
he liked the most, he laughed and said
Hell, they pay me to make 'em, not watch 'em.

Too much podex osculation
going down in Tinseltown to suit Bob.
He wrote wild poems and smoked grass all his life,

paid the LAPD a grand a month not to bust him.
He once rescued Charlie Parker from a dustbin
and he never got too big for his boots.

Hey There

How come you find it acceptable
to watch quiz shows all of a sudden?
There's a simpleton's grin on your fat face –

aren't you paying attention or what?
You scaled Masada once like a gazelle,
now look at you. You're there in your dim room

like a cobweb, like a cup of tea
gone cold. You're there like a bongo
no one ever bangs a rhythm out on.

You remain baffled by the world at large
despite the facts you now love to reel off
such as naming the moons of Uranus.

Afternoon with David

When I turned the corner and spotted him
smiling in the sunshine in his garden
with a cup of tea at a white plastic table

I became unsteady, thrust out a hand
moving sideways more than forward
all in the gasp of a shock then over

and he said 'hi' quite cheerfully
as did I, then sat down across from him
and accepted a brew and piece of cake

and sipped and chewed, marvelled at his laughter
and the fight he was putting up
beneath a parasol as the sun died.

Another Fine Mess

You spent last night with eight comrades
and two coppers, if that stoned type was right
about one in five at any meeting of lefties.

Well, he should know. He looked crazy enough
to play the flute, or write for a living, crazy enough
to sneer at a judge from the dock.

You were scoffing fish 'n' chips by lock gate six
when things went BOOM! You were burnt black, hairless,
rendered quite deaf, and you lost your sense of humour.

Do something to help me! wails Oliver Hardy
down the years, his hopes sinking, his ear
full of milk, his legs tied round his neck.

1970s British Blues

Punching the same ragged riff half to death
the tuning all over the place
he just knew he'd never impress anyone. So

he did a Pete Townshend, which was a hoot,
and taught himself instead to drink eight pints
without losing control of the pool table.

One hot summer he was chased by coppers,
caught in woods and given a fair kicking.
Like but not like a hire purchase agreement.

'Man Who Dug Golf Course Up Had Taken LSD!'
gushed the headline of the *Chronicle*
after the magistrates finished him off.

Trio

He'd be trying to save a butterfly
from a slow death at the bathroom window,
she'd be hanging washing out on the line,
the cat parading round her feet.

That was summer. In the winter
they'd be side by side on the settee,
the cat snoring softly in his lap,
poets and house painters calling all hours.

When rain was belting down, a freezing wind howling,
the cat would stand and stare, furious in the doorway,
before turning to look at him or her as if to say
Are you going to do something about this or what?

Autumn Love Poem

She was coughing again
last night, I couldn't sleep

and sat at our table,
nervous in the moonlight.

Something at the window
was trying to get in,

the moon looked right through me
and made a hollow sound.

The moon once sang and danced,
once told the greatest jokes;

my girl laughed for ever,
my girl and I both laughed.

I'll make some soup, good soup,
stir honey in her tea.

Her clothes hang loose, slip down.
She filled them in the spring.

Heart

Two nurses came, wheeled her away;
the lift door opened, she waved a thin hand,
they went in, disappeared

and I
sat there
with nothing

to do
except
sit there

and time
sat with me
barely

breathing
un
til

I crouch at her bed-side
clutching a mug of tea
she sips from through a straw, flat on her back.

She's off somewhere
with the morphine, wild-eyed.
'Isn't it nice when they like cheese!' she says.

Visiting

When will they cease poking
'n' prodding my darling?
She's had enough. I've had enough.
Better days better be coming.

I tell her Chester's gorilla was seen
bursting his britches again,
lugging a large amount
of rhubarb and lager,

and I missed a bus by seconds
and had to wait for half an hour
at the stop across from
the Freemasons' dive.

The lights were on.
I could detect movement
behind the frosted glass.
It was silent, the whole street was.
No one joined me at the stop.
No one said hello.

Blue Frogs

She had bony fingers
that held a syringe
she used to inject ink
into frogs.
The bloated blue frogs
looked flummoxed,
wobbled round
for a minute or so
before dropping dead.
She laughed and smirked
and laughed and shrieked
and laughed and whooped.
It was a heavy thing

for a little boy to take in.
He watched her stoop
to pick the dead frogs up
one at a time by one leg,
drop them in the dustbin.
He watched her go inside,
shut her door.
He sat on the stone steps,
stared round.
Small pools of ink
dotted the yard.
If he shut his eyes he saw
blue frogs as statues.

66, 67, 68

That year booting a ball
against the panelled steel door
of the post office garage
the great clanging, rippling racket
as the ball whacked against it
all the way to bedtime
Moore to Charlton to Hurst WHACK!
what a bloody goal
that one crossed the line alright
no one ever told you to stop
no one bothered you at all.

*

You were put in a uniform,
waved off to boys' grammar school.
Part of the uniform was a daft cap,
to be worn like a flag of surrender
from leaving home to arriving at school.
Prefects were stationed at odd parts of town
and if you were caught with no cap
you'd be given cap detention,
an hour of writing
'I must wear my cap when travelling to and from school'
over and over.

*

Master of air guitar
Anyway, Anyhow, Anywhere
and other glorious rackets

alone at last, in your room
out of the poxy uniform
after the torture of the day
lurking about all evening
trying it on with Maria V
who half-fancied you because she said
you resembled one of Strawberry Alarm Clock
who you thought were all foul.

Birthday Girl

When I sat down
and wished her a happy birthday
she said birthdays
were nothing to celebrate,
they just reminded you
how much time had gone
and how little was left.
Perhaps she guessed
what was coming –
all the good times done with,
packed away like old hats –
drinking herself senseless
in an absence of fun.

That day, on her thirty-second birthday,
we sat in the sunshine
as tiny birds
hovered round us,
landed right next to us
making a fine racket,
as if demanding an explanation,
or offering one,
if we could only understand.

Bottleneck

He went to a very dark place
his wife tells us, her face like chalk,
and stayed there till the day he died.
We try to picture Pete in his dark place.

A pint or two with Nev before the train
becomes a load of pints and fuck the train.
Remember this, remember that, remember...
It was over thirty years since I last saw Pete -

just the three of us Nev, we were blotto,
we smoked all the hash through a bottleneck,
lay trapped for hours like turtles on our backs.
And watched the sky unzip its cool leather jacket.

Rhino

His door slams shut like a head butt.
He's growling like some beast in a trap.

You creep to the peep-hole, see him lurching
beneath thick rolls of electrical cable.

He's told you more than once he works away, Scotland,
yet every day he's in and out like a rhino.

Once at midnight you stood in this same spot,
watching him crawl along the corridor

drunk as can be, swearing all the way, then
the prolonged agony of the key and the lock...

He has a line of vehicles in the car park.
They're always there. Never in Scotland.

Love Story

It was hard to resist
when he read her message:
Get your arse over here
my ashtray needs emptying.

Seems he was forgiven
for the comments about her dad,
for what remained of her Audi,
for maybe everything.

Come here Darlin', he said,
taking her in his arms
before tripping, straight through
the plate glass living room door.

Red Wings

They were arguing
well no, not even that
just arsing about

but it ended with
Frank's forearm sliced open
down to the bone, elbow to wrist

blood spouting
in all directions, the flesh flapping
like two red wings

a pale witness
throwing up all over
everybody's feet.

If

If all music sounded like the world's angriest hornet
        amplified a thousand times
and if "wheat" did not appear on every packet in our kitchen
        but "trilby" and "vest" did
and if 'My Funeral' was a popular name for a girl
and if dodos weren't extinct but sailors were
and if magpies recited poems in the voice of Noel Coward
and if David Icke was wrong about the lizards
and if Captain Kirk and Mister Spock materialised every time
        you looked in your wardrobe
and if a cat running up a curtain was the basis for the world's
        most popular religion
and if Picasso had died a virgin in a house full of tears
and if people bought so many books they had nowhere to put them
and if pork pies and tobacco turned out in the end to be good for you
and if all the stupid films were brilliant films
and if the Marx Brothers had been called the Hitler Brothers
        and their reputation had waned
and if thoughts and ideas weren't lost if you didn't note them
        but waited for you in the fridge
and if the Prime Minister replied to questions with harmonica solos
and if the moon landings had never happened, or had
and if there was more than one way to outrun a lion
and if the strings of your heart could not be plucked
and if we encountered the under toad at an early age and knew
        when he was coming every time
and if Professor Hard Times and Joe Ignorant were the
        Trotsky and Stalin of British politics
and if 'Once Upon a Time in the West' was set in the East
and if everybody had size fourteen feet
and if a cat running up a curtain was a vital clue

and if the Queen published a lurid sex manual
and if an old school tie was merely something you used
            to choke a bastard
and if we all had to hide in a foreign embassy for ever
            knitting patterned pullovers
and if coming second was better than coming first
and if it was only possible to speak in the present tense
and if no one could ever miss a bus, or catch an undertone
and if people working in fish 'n' chip shops were better off than lawyers
and if you could stare at a boot and find something in it
            and not just a foot
and if we were immortal and God was an abandoned pizza
            with a cigarette crushed out in the crust
and if people still had lives rather than gadgets
and if Tarring Neville was not a village but a procedure
and if Peter, Paul and Mary had been called Dick, Balls and Quim
and if no one spent their life looking for stuff to sniff at
and if *Beat the Devil* was not a movie liked only by phonies
            et moi
and if kicking against the pricks was a degree course
            at Oxford and Cambridge
and if President Oscar Flake made smoking marijuana compulsory
and if a postcard from the seaside was a portent of doom
and if the world's most venomous snake was a pacifist
and if a cat running up a curtain was a cure for cancer
and if the greatest minds of our time all chose television
            game shows as a career
and if birds could only fly backwards and were constantly
            colliding comically
and if ashtrays could be used to replace diseased lungs
and if bicycles were poems and saddlebags field recordings
and if game birds enjoyed being blown to bits in mid-flight
and if you always got a good night's sleep no matter what

and if investment bankers always spoke with their fingers
        stretching each side of their mouth
and if Malcolm X had been white and Bob Dylan had been black
        and still only one had survived the 60s
and if Thelonious Monk was still gigging at the Five Spot
and if one and one made boo and boo and boo made boo hoo
and if something bit you on the leg every time you travelled by train
and if hamsters surprised us by saving the planet
and if the ghosts of Frank Zappa and Bill Hicks were running
        on the Republican ticket
and if Vincent Price and his mother were there to greet us
        at the gates of Paradise
and if a cat running up a curtain was an ingredient in a pie
and if the lines of a poem could be read in any order
and if it was impossible to run out of steam
and if the second world war had been a hen party
then maybe this would be the nation's favourite poem.

In a Hostel

He forgets
his medication
sometimes,
came to this place
for a month
without it.

'It stops me
from wanting
to kill people,'
he says
from the next bed
with the lights out.

Lonely as a Crowd

Nearly Time

It's nearly time for face masks
to be worn at all times by everyone.

It's nearly time to speak
in a false voice, warm and friendly.

It's nearly time to accept
no gifts, or be as lost as you can be.

It's nearly time to bury
your face in your hands behind closed doors and weep.

It's nearly time to milk
your dying cow for all it's worth.

It's nearly time to eat
slices of dry bread like a thief.

It's nearly time for truth
that persists like the sky and the screaming.

It's nearly time to spit
on cherished dreams and their dreamers.

It's nearly time for noises
that glow in the night.

It's nearly time to crawl
through mud in the name of the Lord.

It's nearly time for the wolf
to rise from his grave and collect everything he's owed.

It's nearly time to hold
your breath and cross your fingers hopefully.

It's nearly time to think
of the perfect retort and say it again and again.

It's nearly time for a demijohn
to be the must-have fashion accessory.

It's nearly time for the sun
to start to wax and wane.

It's nearly time for Death
to suggest it had all been a mistake.

It's nearly time to acknowledge
you didn't laugh because you weren't sure it was a joke.

It's nearly time for something real
that cannot be denied.

It's nearly time for God
to find Himself in a giant egg cup, a giant spoon poised above.

It's nearly time
to dip a soldier.

I'm Geoffrey

My dad's nocturnal adventure
with a packed suitcase and muddy bare feet
includes getting picked up at a bus stop
by a young woman in a transit van
who took him to her place, fed him and washed his feet
before handing him over to the police.

*

I'm sitting round with my brothers.
*Clear signs of dementia. We can't
be thinking he might get better. He could
burn the house down, good God*

now he doesn't know who I am.
Says I look a bit like his eldest son, Geoffrey.
That's me, I tell him, I'm Geoffrey.
Don't talk daft, tha too old.

*

My Uncle Bill was no uncle, just my dad's pal.
He dropped dead in the pub while playing pool,
forty-seven. He was wearing a suit and tie.
My dad's standing with him in the garden,
laughing in the sunshine at the same old stories.

In the Springtime

The queue outside the Aldi
spreads all round the car park,
out onto the street and round

the corner where it meets up
with the queue at the bus stop
like a couple on an awkward first date.

I count fifty more or less
socially distanced would-be shoppers
ahead of me, then lose the count.

One person leaves the store,
trolley piled high with pasta,
baked beans and biscuits,

another is waved in by a black girl
with a gap in her front teeth
just like mine and Jimmy Tarbuck's.

A Nigel Farage thinkalike
in front of me turns round
to give me his version of things,

which goes on and on
as the chopping body shuffles forward
like it's not well, forty minutes

and I can only console myself
that it's sunny, no rain,
and I won't live for ever.

Finally I get there, exchanging gaps
with the black girl, finally I'm in there,
but only to find the shelves all but bare.

Some fat git on his mobile:
'It's absolutely mad Susan,
there's not a single chip in t'place.'

No beer, no wine, my God, just the hard stuff,
not much of that. A bottle of dark rum
catches my eye, wins me over.

There are bog rolls across the road
in the newsagents, I overhear,
but not by the time I get there.

Home at Last

The fortieth day of my house arrest.
I fall asleep so easily – not once
have I got through 'Murder Most Foul'.

I sang the phrase "Well, the" hundreds of times
day after day for a week. I got dead good at it.
I'm working on "danger on the rocks" now.

*

It seemed a bad time to visit A & E
but it was deserted. I was the sole patient,
limping along the gleaming corridor like a three-legged dog.

I have to elevate my foot, sit with it up
till it gets better. Which should be a few weeks.
Which will pass like decades of misery.

*

Oh to be in a hot country,
guzzling moonshine on a ganja plantation,
an honoured guest, welcomed

for my knowledge of polyrhythms
and the poetics of alienation
and loads of other fibs.

Neighbours

Him with the tattoos and weekend children –
once told me he used to play in Bad Seeds
and still gets Christmas cards
from Nick Cave – they're bundling him
cursing into a police van,
a couple of the coppers dripping wet.

Her with the daft old dog and winged glasses
says it's the funniest thing she's seen in ages.
They walked up to him – "You're nicked!"
Then he shoved them in the canal, just like that.
They landed in the middle of all these ducks,
flapping their arms and screaming blue murder.

Going up in the lift
with her with the bald patch
who doesn't have it now
I hear it's all about drugs,
a burglary at the Chemist's.
I don't say I believe her, I don't say I don't.

On the third floor
the smell of weed
almost knocks me out.
'I hate that smell,'
says her with the bum-brushing ponytail,
'if I'm not part of it.'

The Effort

He wakes slowly
from a dream of childhood,
a dream of strength
and a sense of purpose,
a dream full of wishes
that might come true,
plans for tomorrow
and the day after.

He sits drinking water
and not smoking a cigarette
at three o'clock in the morning.

He once stopped for two days
but it was a mistake –
he ran out of money
in a hostile city -
had to hitch a lift back,
making small talk
as his head spun
from the effort of not smoking.

He sits scratching his chin
and not smoking a cigarette
at four o'clock in the morning.

The guy behind the wheel
had said, *Howdy, partner,*
I'm from Austin, Texas,
and started banging on
about armadillos,

whose vile eating habits
include a taste
for maggot-ridden flesh.

He sits tapping his fingers
and not smoking a cigarette
at five o'clock in the morning.

This Flat

This flat is where music comes home to chill,
where clouds fill the windows with great notions,
this flat is where light gathers and dances,
where herons and kestrels and owls say Hi.

This flat was made to be paced in deep thought
and to resound with the gift of laughter,
the perfect place to stand and say out loud
'Who cares what a bunch of nitwits might think?'

This flat is a top spot to get blotto,
to greet the crack of dawn with a good swig,
this flat is like a poem fighting to live,
to get out there in the world and frolic.

Winter Lockdown Blues

Amber warning, heavy snow, sub zero.
Nothing to do but climb the wall, listen to something low.

Full white car park, part buried cars, spots of movement.
Dogs in bright coats, a scaredy cat, wrapped up humans.

I hope there's plenty to eat in the house.

A young woman, maybe twenty, striding along.
Blue jeans, red vest, sandals, mane of black hair

stuck to her back. She couldn't be wetter.
She looks good, (did I take my

seven o'clock tablet?) psychotic but good.

Sometimes I get so desperate I recollect
something in me tired of turning the other cheek.

Tomorrow Never Knows

I dreamt I was Ringo Starr's mate,
dishing up beans on toast
all hours of the day and night –

Ringo, I said, am I losing my mind,
or have we in fact been taken over
by an alien species?

Sometimes a dream continues on another night.
I'm hoping that's the case with this.
In my favourite dream, the one where

I have absolute power, Boris Johnson Night
has replaced Guy Fawkes Night
and the firework displays are dead feisty.

No Comfort Zone

Pressure is now the norm, we're under it always,
even fetching supplies can end up touch and go.

I feel old, take my time, heavy bags in each hand.
A youth on a doorstep sneers and spits at my feet.

A few facial repairs required just for starters.
Only three teeth left now and they don't meet.

My snore, I'm told, sounds like a death rattle
at the bottom of a deep pit.

Twenty years since I did anything to shout about.
Charity shops are where I exist now.

I yearn to fry an egg and a slice of white bread,
smother them in salt and get stuck in.

Wizened

Wheezing like a wizened ex-miner
on the cold streets of South Yorkshire in the '60s –
why are the hills so steep? They never were before.

I find my friend in his usual chair.
He sits whittling on the same piece of wood;
it goes nowhere and will always arrive.

He's a heavy drinker, compulsive gambler,
terrible womaniser – he'll admit it, adding
he's got his faults as well of course.

He doesn't mind religious folk
if they don't mind him. He knows the Joke Police
are cracking down; his lips remain unzipped.

Lonely as a Shroud

Simply to limp along
like a half-starved stray cat
all the way to the bottle bank

can feel like a triumph
after waking from a nightmare
of Karen Carpenter on a slab in the morgue,

her bare-knuckle take on 'Barstool Blues'
breaking hearts from a last legs jukebox –
you never saw anybody deader.

You love the racket when bottles shatter,
chucking them in one at a time,
your face a mask, man in control.

Lonely as a Crowd

The Trump's pompous, petulant face
coldly peering as I chew my corn flakes.
He says his ratings are out of this world,
or did he say ravings? I say he did.

I was trapped for some time last night
with a highly-rated saxophonist
who fell hard for the one about Ornette Coleman
taking a razor to his balls. A gullible nitwit,

full of himself and thick and misogynistic.
"What a knobhead!" I heard one woman say,
in fact it was my wife. "What a total - "
Highly-rated. Big fat white guy. Sold out.

Mostly Bob

It must be strange to be so close
to retirement, and still not know
what you want to be when you grow up.

At least you've got old Bob, young Bob,
middle-aged Bob, all the Bobs
to help you with the long dark nights.

I know it's not just Bob, but it *is* mostly Bob.
There's no need to sulk, it could be far worse.
It could be a much bleaker scenario in many ways.

So you went to the doctor's and you're OK?
You're OK except for your heart?
No, not your heart, your brain?

Hatter'sley

Someone offering to set fire to you
for next to nowt, someone raising money
for bloody dogs, a catalogue of disasters

waiting to occur, all the way from bowel cancer
to losing your marbles, eating 'teasted toecakes'
for breakfast, keeping your collection of beermats

and matchboxes in a 'boardcard box',
signing your name with an apostrophe
in front of the s and feeling smart for doing it.

Your wife hands you a list and you walk to the shop.
You are required to purchase, just in case of emergency, bacon,
and you can see the wisdom of that.

Mondegreens

Not elegant trump
elephant gun

Not that fried egg feeling
that Friday feeling

Not her favourite psychopath
cycle path

Not Josey Wales
save the whales

Not hey typical
atypical

Not pig-faced angular rough shark
squid

Smart Patches

Goodbye toe fungus
hello holiday homes

a Japanese scientist has discovered something
frozen pies

reduce your wrinkles
get rid of turkey neck once and for all

this is the place where germs will thrive
beautiful Asian women want older men

primer and foundation
shoes to conquer the world

Japanese smart patches
before you go to bed

Michael Goes Missing

Six months after you were thrown out of art college
you stayed on this Balearic island
for more than a week, less than a month,
there was a hippy artists colony there,
out of their heads from all the hash cookies
they munched on continually, sculptors and painters
and what have you, music generated
by large windpipes catching the breeze
and the surf's relentless rhythm.

Then there was Istanbul, hiding there
in the world's shittiest hotel.
There was Karachi, the worst meat
you've ever had in your mouth in your life.
There was a giant pan, burnt black, steaming.
India was more like it, in the streets
people were everywhere making music.
You bought some bongos, yoghurt and a flute.
You could see things, smell things, something in you

breaks apart then reassembles smartly,
you hitch a ride in a very small car crammed with carpets
and you get all the way to the Bulgarian border
and the driver doesn't have the papers for the car.
You know this is crazy. That first night
you sleep in a pumpkin field, and you wake up
and there's a guy pointing a rifle at you.
What am I doing here? you ask yourself.
You could well be the first black man he's met.

You're here for saying no, I shall not kill
Vietnamese people for you.
It's not a joke but seems kind of funny.
You look up and see the pale moon
hanging on for dear life.
They're talking about walking on it soon.
You take a breath. 'Hey, can you speak English?'

Coming Clean

I'm too honest for my own good
which is why I lie all the time
and why everyone knows I lie
and no one thinks I'm not lying
nor do I pretend not to be lying
therefore that's not really a lie
if it's so transparently a lie
so yes, that is, no no, I did not lie
and if I did I didn't know I was
except when I did, but listen
I'd be lying if I told you
there are people out there who believe me
and there are people out there who believe me
believe it or not and I put it to you
truth, lies, what's the difference
I am a man of honesty, integrity
a true lie for every occasion, mm
bear with me, I had my hair trimmed for this
I just need to lie about a few more things
before I go, not that I'm going anywhere
I am who I am and should be
rightly adored.

Warehouse

My dad would be shaving
by five; I'd shaved
the night before.
I'd make a pot of tea,
sit hands round mug
in my blue overall.

We drove to work
in silence, more or less;
he was hard-of-hearing
from the steelworks -
fifteen long years then just like that
no more steelworks.

In the army
he'd driven officers
from A to B, still had the air
of that driver.
He kept his eyes on the road,
smart remarks to himself.

Now seen as a good worker,
moved up from the warehouse
to operations planning.
When we got there, walked through the door,
he'd disappear down his hole
and I down mine.

Space

It's not true that people like me.
OK, it's true sometimes
but mostly not. They don't like me
and I often can't stand the sight of them.

To be with my wife is enough for me,
just to occupy the same space.

She's engrossed in *The Invasion*
which is, she claims, a cracking read
about the gentrification of working class areas.

What gets her most is the indifference.
I think at times that gets me most as well.
Times like today, yesterday, tomorrow.

Acknowledgements

Thanks are due to the editors of the following publications, where some of these poems, or versions of them, have previously appeared: *The Echo Room*, *The North*, *The Slab*, *Pennine Platform*, *Melville's D.A.* (US), *Judas-hole*, *Schizzo*, *Fool-saint*, *Proletarian Poetry*, *Clear Poetry*, and *Poetry Birmingham Literary Journal.*

The author would like to thank The Royal Literary Fund for gainful employment during the period most of these poems were written. Thanks also to Ed Reiss, David Spencer, Philip Foster, Julia Deakin, and John Sugden, and thanks and rest in peace to Mark Hinchliffe, Milner Place, and David Kennedy. Thanks especially and love always to Jeanette Hattersley.

LAY OUT YOUR UNREST